Ecuador
Peru
Bolivia

country	area sq mi (sq km)	population (1995)	capital	currency
ECUADOR	109,490 (283,557)	10,891,000	Quito	Sucre
PERU	496,260 (1,285,214)	24,087,000	Lima	Sol
BOLIVIA	424,195 (1,098,580)	7,896,000	La Paz	Boliviano

PACIFIC
OCEAN

0   200 mi

400 km

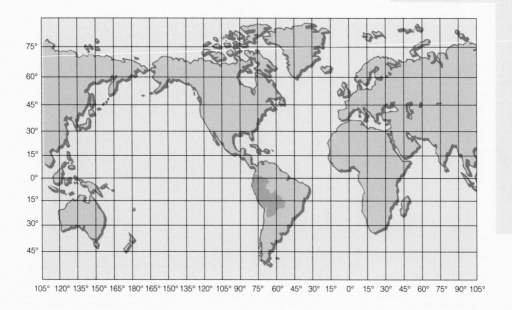

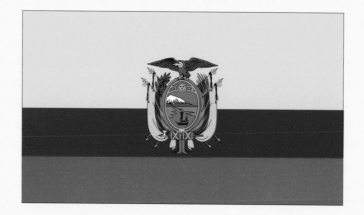

Ecuador

Peru

Bolivia

Ecuador
Peru
Bolivia

Edward Parker

RSVP

RAINTREE
STECK-VAUGHN
P U B L I S H E R S

The Steck-Vaughn Company

Austin, Texas

Published by Raintree Steck-Vaughn Publishers, an imprint of Steck-Vaughn Company

Design and typesetting Roger Kohn Designs
Commissioning editor Hazel Songhurst
Editor Merle Thompson
Assistant editor Diana Russell
Picture research Shelley Noronha
Maps János Márffy

We are grateful to the following for permission to reproduce photographs:
Front Cover: J. Horner *above*;
Getty Images *below* (Ed Simpson);
B. Coleman, page 43 (Gunter Ziesler); Getty Images, pages 10/11 (Kevin Schafer), 11 *below* (Robin Smith); Robert Harding, page 37; Jeremy Horner, page 39 *below*; Image Bank, page 18 (P & G Bowater); Impact, pages 20 *above* (Michael Mirecki), 22 *right* (Colin Jones), 24 (Michael Mirecki), 27 (Piers Cavendish), 28 (Robert Gibbs), 35 *left* (Robert Gibbs), 38 (Alastair Indge); Tony Morrison, pages 9, 12 *above*, 13, 14, 19 *above* and *below*, 20 *below*, 30 *above* (Robert Francis), 30 *below*, 41 *above*; NHPA, page 40 (Kevin Schafer); Edward Parker, pages 8 *above* and *below*, 12 *below*, 15 *above* and *below*, 16, 17, 21, 22 *left*, 23, 25 *above* and *below*, 31, 32 *left*, 32/33, 34 *left*, 35 *right*, 39 *above*, 44 *above*; Rex Features, page 29 *left* (Wesley Bocxe); Still Pictures, pages 26 *above* and *below*, (Mark Edwards), 29 *above* (John Maier), 36 (Mark Edwards), 41 *below* (Mark Edwards), 44 *below* (Chris Caldicott); Harry Trusted, page 43.

The statistics given in this book are the most up-to-date available at the time of going to press.

Printed in Hong Kong by Wing King Tong

Library of Congress Cataloging-in-Publication Data
Parker, Edward, 1961–
Ecuador, Peru, and Bolivia / Edward Parker.
p.   cm. — (Country fact files)
Includes bibliographical references and index.
Summary: Introduces the landscape, climate, natural resources, people, and culture of Ecuador, Peru, and Bolivia.
ISBN 0-8172-5403-X
1. Ecuador — Juvenile literature.   2. Peru — Juvenile literature.   3. Bolivia — Juvenile literature.   [1. Ecuador. 2. Peru.   3. Bolivia.]   I. Title.   II. Series.
F3708.5.P37   1998
980 — dc21   97-40241
                                    CIP   AC

1 2 3 4 5 6 7 8 9 0 HK 01 00 99 98 97

CONTENTS

Words that are explained in the glossary are printed in
SMALL CAPITALS the first time they are mentioned in the text.

INTRODUCTION

Ecuador, Peru, and Bolivia lie on the western side of South America. Together they cover almost 1.04 million square miles (2.7 million sq km), or about 15 percent of the continent's total land area. That's a quarter of the size of the United States.

If you ask people what they know about these countries, some may mention the ancient Inca civilization. Others will speak of local people playing haunting panpipe music. Many will talk of the soaring, snow-capped Andes Mountains, steamy tropical forests, and sun-baked deserts. They may also discuss the severe social problems and turbulent political history of the region. However, there are many more points of interest in these countries, each of which has its own distinct character.

Long before the first Europeans arrived there, great civilizations developed in the region. Between 1400 B.C. and A.D. 1532, many cultures flourished, such as the Nazca of the Peruvian Desert, the Tiahuanaco-Huari of the highlands of Bolivia, and the Incas.

The Incas built large cities, massive stone temples and palaces, and a major network of roads. Theirs was a highly organized society. At its peak the Inca empire stretched north beyond Ecuador into Colombia, and south and east through Bolivia into Chile and Argentina.

In the 16th century, rumors of gold and other riches attracted the Spanish to the area. They

▲ *This stone carving of a warrior belongs to the Chavin culture, which flourished on the western slopes of the Andes between 1300 and 400 B.C.*

▲ *About half the population of all three countries continue to live in the Andes, growing their food in gardens such as this one in Ecuador.*

conquered the Incas and ruled there for about 300 years. After a violent colonial history, all three countries fought for and gained independence from Spain in the early 19th century.

Today Ecuador, Peru, and Bolivia are countries of great contrasts. In each one, there are wealthy and cosmopolitan cities, but there are also areas where many people live in conditions of great poverty, with few schools and hospitals.

▼ *La Paz is the capital of Bolivia and the highest capital city in the world. Its central plaza stands at an altitude of 11,929 feet (3,636 m). The snow-covered peak of Mount Illimani is 21,003 feet (6,402 m) and towers over the city.*

ECUADOR, PERU, AND BOLIVIA AT A GLANCE

● Population (1995): 7,896,254 in Bolivia; 10,890,950 in Ecuador; 24,087,372 in Peru
● Capitals: La Paz (Bolivia), population 715,000; Quito (Ecuador) 1.29 million; Lima (Peru) 5.71 million
● Highest mountain: Huascarán (Peru), 22,204 feet (6,768 m)
● Longest river: Amazon, 4,050 miles (6,516 km)
● Languages: Spanish, Quechua, Aymara
● Major religions: Roman Catholicism, traditional beliefs
● Currency: Boliviano (Bolivia), written as $B1 ($B1 = 100 centavos); sucre (Ecuador), written as 1S/ (1S/ = 100 centavos); nuevo sol (Peru), written as 1S/ (1S/ = 100 centimos)
● Major resources: Fish, wood, silver, copper, lead, tin, oil, gas
● Major exports: FISH MEAL, oil, bananas, shrimp, coffee, fruit, cotton, textiles, wood, minerals
● Environmental problems: Soil erosion, DEFORESTATION, water and air pollution

THE LANDSCAPE

The region formed by Ecuador, Peru, and Bolivia has a very varied landscape. It includes mountains covered in snow, tropical beaches, parched deserts, luxuriant rain forests, and bleak, windswept plateaus.

Peru and Bolivia lie south of the equator, which cuts across Ecuador just north of the capital, Quito. Peru and Ecuador are bordered on the west by the Pacific Ocean, while Bolivia has no coastline. The region has frontiers with Colombia, Brazil, Paraguay, Argentina, and Chile.

The three countries stand on a part of the

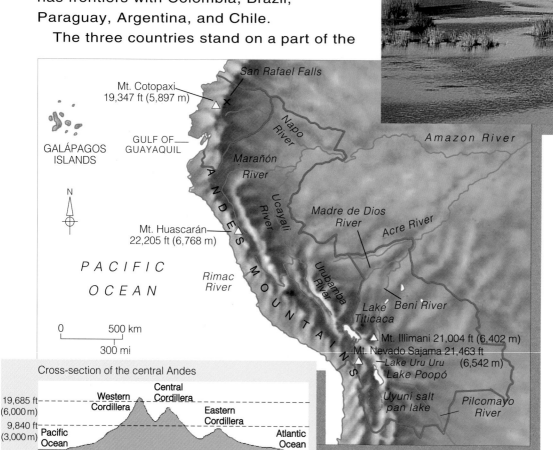

Mt. Cotopaxi 19,347 ft (5,897 m)

San Rafael Falls

GALÁPAGOS ISLANDS

GULF OF GUAYAQUIL

Napo River

Marañón River

Ucayali River

Amazon River

Madre de Dios River

Acre River

N

Mt. Huascarán 22,205 ft (6,768 m)

PACIFIC OCEAN

Rimac River

Urubamba River

ANDES MOUNTAINS

0   500 km
    300 mi

Lake Titicaca

Beni River

Mt. Illimani 21,004 ft (6,402 m)
Mt. Nevado Sajama 21,463 ft
Lake Uru Uru   (6,542 m)
Lake Poopó

Uyuni salt pan lake

Pilcomayo River

Cross-section of the central Andes

19,685 ft (6,000 m)
9,840 ft (3,000 m)

Western Cordillera

Central Cordillera

Eastern Cordillera

Pacific Ocean

Atlantic Ocean

▲ *Small boats can often be seen navigating the reeds on Lake Titicaca. The Uros people traditionally build their homes on "floating islands" on the lake. These are artificial islands made out of reeds.*

Earth's crust where there is a GEOLOGICAL FAULT. This means that there are many powerful volcanoes there, and earthquakes hit the region several times each century.

The region is dominated by the Andes mountain range, which runs approximately northwest to southeast. The Andes are made up of "cordilleras," or ranges, which are roughly parallel to one another. In Peru, there are three—the Western, Central, and Eastern cordilleras.

The Andean region gradually widens as you travel south. Only 62 miles (100 km) wide in Ecuador, the range is 186 miles (300 km) wide by the time you reach

Bolivia. Many peaks are over 19,685 feet (6,000 m) high.

Between the mountain ranges are the high plains known as "puna" or, around Lake Titicaca, ALTIPLANO. They are 9,840 to 14,760 feet (3,000 to 4,500 m) high. These areas are well suited to agriculture and are the traditional home of the rural Andean population. Only in southern Bolivia do the high fertile valleys give way to deserts.

Ecuador's coastline consists of a narrow belt of low-lying land covered in tropical vegetation. It is no more than 62 miles (100 km) at its widest. An even narrower strip of land forms Peru's coastal region between the Andes and the Pacific. Rarely more than 31 miles (50 km) wide, it is a

▶ *The western slopes of the Andes in Peru are rugged deserts where little is able to grow, apart from cacti.*

KEY FACTS

● Peru's Colca Canyon is the world's deepest canyon. It is over 6,560 feet (2,000 m)—twice as deep as the Grand Canyon in the United States.
● Lake Titicaca is the world's highest navigable lake at 12,480 feet (3,805 m).
● At 19,347 feet (5,897 m), Cotopaxi (Ecuador) is the highest active volcano in the world.

barren desert with only 50 small OASES along its entire 1,490-mile (2,400-km) length.

The eastern sectors of all three countries are covered by lowland tropical rain forest. This accounts for two-thirds of Bolivia's total land area. These lands have very low population densities.

South America's longest river, the Amazon, has its source in Peru close to the Pacific coast, but flows more than 3,730 miles (6,000 km) east across Brazil to the Atlantic. Only 2,124 miles (3,419 km) actually pass through Peru. The longest river that flows entirely through the region is the Ucayali (1,100 miles/1,771 km). Ecuador's longest river is the Napo, which forms one of the Amazon's principal northern TRIBUTARIES.

Bolivia has two great river systems. One is the Pilcomayo River, which flows south into Paraguay, where it joins the Paraguay River. The other is formed by ten major rivers, including the Acre, Madre de Dios, and Beni, which flow north, draining into the Amazon Basin. The largest lake in the region is Lake Titicaca, covering an area of 3,140 square miles (8,135 sq km).

▶ *The spectacular 475-foot (145-m) San Rafael Falls in the eastern foothills of the Andes. This is Ecuador's largest waterfall. It is surrounded by rain forest.*

◀ *Destruction caused by an earthquake in the town of Baeza, Ecuador, in 1987. All three countries suffer from occasional earthquakes and volcanic eruptions.*

CLIMATE AND WEATHER

The region lies mainly between the equator and the Tropic of Capricorn, but its climate is chiefly influenced by two other factors—the altitude of the land, and the currents of the Pacific Ocean.

Two types of currents affect the weather of Ecuador and Peru. One is cold and the

▲ Covered in snow, Mount Huayna rises up behind llamas grazing on the altiplano grasslands near Potosí, Bolivia.

other is warm. When the ocean is colder than the land, rain falls over the ocean; but when the ocean is warmer, the coastal areas experience heavy rainfall.

Ecuador is influenced by the warm equatorial countercurrent, which creates a hot and rainy season from January to April. There is heavy rain (over 27.5 in/700 mm in the first three months), and it is very hot, averaging more than 86°F (30°C). From May to December, the cool Humboldt Current from the south dictates the weather. Generally it is slightly cooler, and it rarely rains.

The rain forest area of Ecuador east of the Andes is hot and wet all year, although temperatures are a little lower than those on the coast. However, the Andean region

KEY FACTS

● When EL NIÑO hit Peru in 1993, many areas in the north received 6.5 feet (2 m) of rain in 2 months.
● A cold wind from Argentina occasionally blows over Bolivia's lowland rain forest from May to October, reducing temperatures to nearly freezing.
● Between June and August, altiplano areas above 13,125 feet (4,000 m) in Peru and Bolivia can have nighttime temperatures as low as -13°F (-25°C).

itself has a temperate climate, with a dry season between June and September. The highest mountain peaks, such as Cotopaxi, remain snowcapped all year long.

Peru has three distinct climatic zones: the coastal strip, the Andean region, and the eastern sector. In the coastal strip, the weather is controlled by the cold Humboldt Current. This ensures that very little rain falls, so most of the coast is a drab and barren desert. During the winter (May to November), a damp mist called the GARÚA rolls over most of the coastal cities, keeping temperatures down to only 55–63°F (13–17°C), compared with 68–79°F (20–26°C) in the summer. Every five to ten years, a warm current called El Niño replaces the cold Humboldt Current. The effect is devastating. The change from a cold to a warm ocean causes torrential

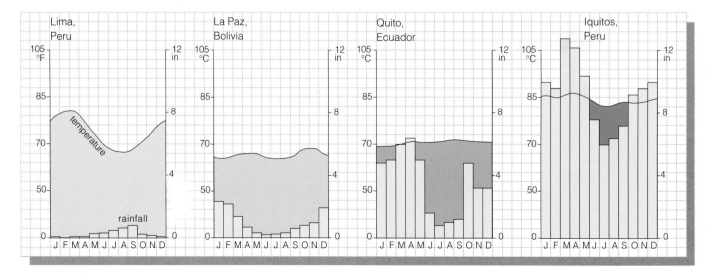

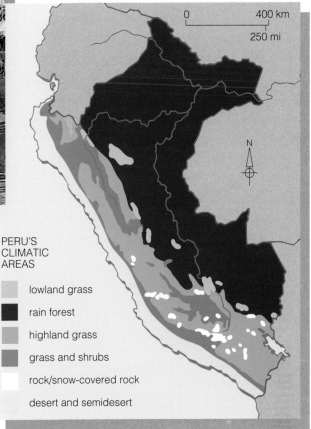

◀ *Peru's coastal strip receives so little rain that very few plants can survive there.*

▲ *A typical coastal village situated along the lush, tropical coastline of Ecuador*

PERU'S CLIMATIC AREAS

- lowland grass
- rain forest
- highland grass
- grass and shrubs
- rock/snow-covered rock
- desert and semidesert

rains to fall over the desert, rather than out to sea. A few feet of rain may fall on the coastal strip in less than a month, bringing floods and landslides.

In Peru's Andean region, the altitude determines the climate. It is generally temperate in the high valleys, while the higher peaks are always covered in snow. Mountains such as Huascarán have glaciers. By contrast, the country's eastern sector, with its tropical rain forest, is hot and wet all year round.

Bolivia also has a wide range of climatic conditions. Winter frosts occur almost everywhere, occasionally even in the lowland tropical forests. In the summer (November to March), there is widespread heavy rain. Around Lake Titicaca, temperatures can quickly fall by 30 degrees within just a few hours.

However, the country's eastern rain forest is typically humid and hot, with heavy rains during most of the year. The average temperature is close to 77°F (25°C), and total rainfall is about 118 inches (3,000 mm) a year.

◀ *Heavy rain falling on the town of Pucalpa in Peru's Amazon rain forest means that the streets can quickly become flooded.*

NATURAL RESOURCES

Ecuador, Peru, and Bolivia have always been rich in natural resources. An abundance of fish enabled large civilizations to develop along the coast more than 2,000 years ago. Amazonian peoples flourished in the species-rich rain forest. And gold, silver, and copper have been mined for over 1,000 years. These metals were used by cultures such as the Chimu, Nazca, and Inca to adorn their temples and palaces, and their availability later attracted Europeans to the region.

Minerals are still very important, especially for the economies of Peru and Bolivia. Peru is one of the most important mining countries in the world—it is the third-largest producer of silver and the seventh-largest producer of copper. The country has big deposits of iron, lead, and gold, too. The iron output is the fastest-rising sector of the mining economy.

Bolivia also relies heavily on its mineral wealth. The export of metals accounts for 39% of all export earnings. In addition to

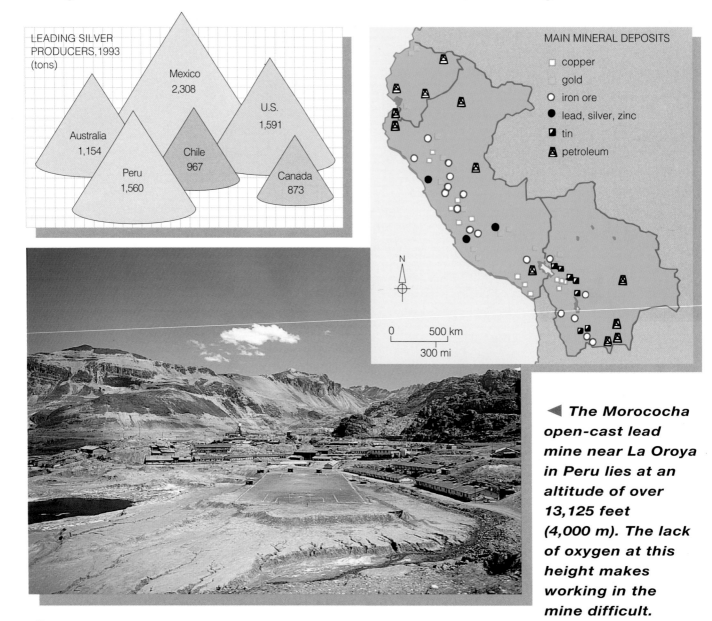

LEADING SILVER PRODUCERS, 1993 (tons)

Mexico 2,308
U.S. 1,591
Australia 1,154
Chile 967
Peru 1,560
Canada 873

MAIN MINERAL DEPOSITS

- □ copper
- ▫ gold
- ○ iron ore
- ● lead, silver, zinc
- ◨ tin
- ⛟ petroleum

0   500 km
300 mi

◀ The Morococha open-cast lead mine near La Oroya in Peru lies at an altitude of over 13,125 feet (4,000 m). The lack of oxygen at this height makes working in the mine difficult.

lead, zinc, and iron, Bolivia has deposits of rare metals such as tin, antimony, tungsten, mercury, silver, and gold.

Ecuador does not have the same wealth of metals as Bolivia and Peru, but it does have large oil and gas reserves. Oil and gas were first discovered in 1917 close to the coast. It was not until the 1970s that the large reserves in the Ecuadorean Amazon were first exploited, and oil fields in the rain-forested eastern part of the country have also been developed. The oil is transported along the TransAndean pipeline over the Andes to the deep-water port of Esmeraldas. Oil is now Ecuador's largest export, accounting for 39% of its exports.

◀ *Crops such as potatoes have been an important resource in the Andes for centuries. They formed the staple diet of ancient cultures such as the Tiahuanaco and the Incas. Today the genes of wild varieties of potatoes and tomatoes are being manipulated by scientists. They are breeding high-yielding varieties to grow commercially all over the world.*

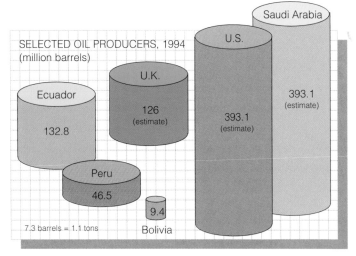

SELECTED OIL PRODUCERS, 1994
(million barrels)

Saudi Arabia
393.1
(estimate)

U.S.
393.1
(estimate)

U.K.
126
(estimate)

Ecuador
132.8

Peru
46.5

9.4
Bolivia

7.3 barrels = 1.1 tons

Peru has been exploiting relatively small quantities of oil in its northern deserts for many years. More recent exploration in the Amazon rain forest region has led to the discovery of vast oil and gas deposits, including one of the world's biggest fields of natural gas, the Camisea. Extensive FOSSIL FUEL reserves have recently been discovered in the Bolivian rain forest, too, and natural gas is becoming one of Bolivia's most important exports.

In the cities, electricity and gas are widely used for fuel. However, a large number of the population lives in rural locations and relies on firewood for cooking and heating. The rivers coursing

▲ **Exploration for oil and natural gas is being carried out in the rain forest areas of all three countries, often by using mobile drilling platforms.**

down the steep slopes of the Andes are used to produce electricity, and there are many hydroelectric plants in all three countries. Today these plants produce 53 percent of Bolivia's electricity and an estimated 70 percent in Ecuador.

An unusual mineral deposit found on the islands just off the coast of Peru led to great wealth in the 19th century. This is GUANO (the accumulation of seabird droppings), which is rich in phosphates. Guano is still collected today from the Ballestas Islands, located just south of Lima. It is used as a

KEY FACTS

● The Camisea gas field near Cuzco in Peru contains an estimated more than three quadrillion metric feet of natural gas — seven times larger than the country's previously known total reserves of oil, gas, and coal.
● There are more than 20,000 species of plants in Ecuador, compared with 17,000 in all of North America.

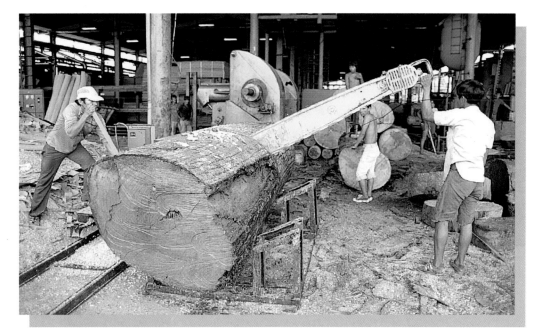

▶ *Some tropical hardwoods are very valuable. Bolivia has great potential for timber production. In 1992 exports of cut timber earned the country US$ 46 million.*

fertilizer for local agriculture, although it is less important than it used to be.

Fish are another key local resource for Peru and Ecuador. The coastal waters of Peru form one of the world's most important fisheries, although this can be disrupted by climate conditions.

The eastern areas of all three countries are heavily forested. Products such as rubber, Brazil nuts, and quinine (a medicine obtained from the bark of cinchona trees) have been harvested for more than 100 years. However, some areas of the rain forest are being rapidly cut down for logging, cattle ranching, and farming, which has led to serious deforestation.

The region's landscapes have become important natural resources for another reason, too. The rugged beauty and the sheer variety of plants and animals attract people from all over the world, and tourism is becoming increasingly important. However, in some areas such as the Galápagos Islands, 620 miles (1,000 km) off the Ecuadorean coast, tourism has to be restricted to protect the environment.

◀ *This is one of the boats of the Peruvian anchovy fishing fleet returning to the port of Chimbote. Chimbote is Peru's main fishing port and the center of the fish meal industry.*

POPULATION

ORIGINS OF THE POPULATIONS

The modern populations of Ecuador, Peru, and Bolivia are descended from the area's INDIGENOUS inhabitants (known as "Indians") and from Europeans.

The arrival of the Spanish in the 16th century had a dramatic effect on local populations. Millions of indigenous people died of newly introduced diseases such as smallpox, to which they had no resistance. Others died after being forced to work as slaves in mines and on plantations. Bolivia's mercury mines were especially deadly—their toxic fumes meant that miners survived only a few years there.

During the colonial period, which lasted about 300 years, large numbers of Europeans arrived in the region, and cities such as Lima and Quito began to grow rapidly. Many European men married local women. Their descendants are known as "MESTIZOS." This group of people now makes up 55% of the population in Ecuador, 37% in Peru, and 30% in Bolivia.

Small sections of the population are descended from black slaves who were brought to the area by Europeans to work

▲ *Bolivian Indians, wearing their distinctive ponchos and bowler hats, walk down the crowded city streets of La Paz.*

▼ *These houses in Bolivia are made of stone and adobe (mud-brick) walls. The building techniques used in rural areas today are not very different from those used in Inca times.*

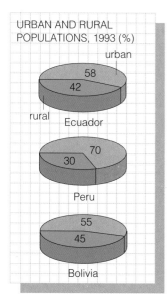

URBAN AND RURAL POPULATIONS, 1993 (%)

urban

58
42

rural Ecuador

70
30

Peru

55
45

Bolivia

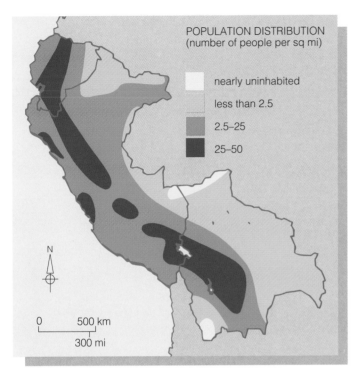

POPULATION DISTRIBUTION
(number of people per sq mi)

- nearly uninhabited
- less than 2.5
- 2.5–25
- 25–50

N

0   500 km

300 mi

POPULATIONS OF THE MAIN CITIES					
ECUADOR (1990 estimate)		**PERU** (1993 census)		**BOLIVIA** (1992 census)	
Guayaquil	1,764,000	Lima	5,710,000	La Paz	715,000
Quito	1,287,000	Callao	640,000	Santa Cruz	700,000
Cuenca	227,000	Arequipa	619,000	Cochabamba	400,000
Machala	166,000	Trujillo	509,000	El Alto	395,000
		Chiclayo	412,000		

accounting for about 55 percent of the country's total. Most of the indigenous people live on the altiplano and speak either Aymara or Quechua. Forty-five percent of Peruvians are Indian, but only a quarter of Ecuador's population is Indian. More than half of all Ecuadoreans are mestizo.

In Bolivia and Ecuador, relatively small

on the plantations, and from Chinese people who arrived to work on the railroads. At the beginning of the 20th century, thousands of Japanese also migrated to the region.

TODAY'S POPULATIONS

The combined populations of Ecuador, Peru, and Bolivia total approximately 43 million people—less than that of the U.K., in a region ten times the U.K.'s size.

The makeup of each country is quite different in terms of population density, ethnic mix, and the size of the urban and rural populations. For example, Bolivia has the lowest population density of any country in South America, while Ecuador has the highest figure in the continent.

Bolivia also has the highest Indian population of any South American country,

▶ *The Tsatchila Indians (called "Colorado" by the Spanish) live in Ecuador's lowland rain forest. They are distinctive because of the red paste they use in their hair.*

numbers of Indians live in the rain forest. However, in Peru the rain forest Indian population is estimated at between 200,000 and 250,000.

MIGRATION

During the 20th century, the populations of all three countries have become much more urban. More than half of all Bolivians and Ecuadoreans now live in towns and cities. In Peru the figure is about 70 percent.

Since the 1950s the extreme poverty suffered by many people in the rural Andes has led to a mass migration toward the coast, especially the cities. Many young people leave the countryside in search of work. This trend increased during the 1970s and 1980s, when terrorist groups such as "Sendero Luminoso" (Shining Path) were active in the countryside. The migration from the Andes to the coastal cities has slowed since the early 1990s, partially because terrorist activities have almost ceased in the Andes.

More recently there has been increasing migration of people from the Andes to the

◀ *Quito is the second largest city in Ecuador after the port of Guayaquil. In the old part of the city, people gather on weekends and holidays in squares such as the Plaza Santa Domingo.*

▲ *The riverside houses of Iquitos (in the Peruvian rain forest) are built on stilts, because water levels there can rise rapidly. Iquitos is Peru's largest rain forest town, and the main commercial center of the Amazon region.*

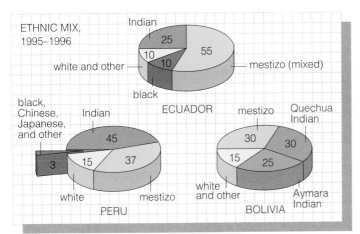

ETHNIC MIX, 1995–1996

Indian
25
white and other
10
10
55 — mestizo (mixed)
black
ECUADOR

black, Chinese, Japanese, and other
Indian
45
3
15
37
white
mestizo
PERU

mestizo
Quechua Indian
30
30
15
25
white and other
Aymara Indian
BOLIVIA

rain-forested lowlands. This has been most notable in Bolivia, where land is being cleared for new plantations and small farms.

POPULATION GROWTH

The populations of all three countries have grown rapidly this century. The growth rate

▶ *Students at a college in Arequipa, Peru, reflect the varied ethnic mix of the region's population.*

KEY FACTS

● About 45% of Peru's population speak Quechua as their first language, while 25% of the people in Bolivia speak Aymara as their first language.

● In 1531 the Inca empire covered a larger area than the Roman empire at its height.

● The region's population density averages just over 41 people per square mile — compared with 67 in the United States, 849 in Japan, and 1,606 in Europe.

● Alberto Fujimori, who became president of Peru in 1990, is descended from Japanese migrants who arrived in the country at the beginning of the 20th century.

● The first people to live in the region are thought to have arrived from Asia around 12,000 B.C.

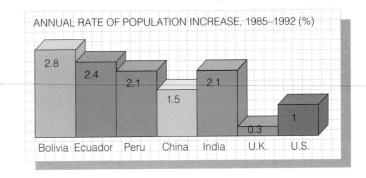

ANNUAL RATE OF POPULATION INCREASE, 1985–1992 (%)

Bolivia	Ecuador	Peru	China	India	U.K.	U.S.
2.8	2.4	2.1	1.5	2.1	0.3	1

is now slowing down. In 1995 Ecuador, Peru, and Bolivia had growth rates of 2.3%, 1.9%, and 2.0% respectively. However, more than a third of the region's total population is under 15 years of age. This is a high figure compared with the U.K. (17%) and the U.S. (22%).

FAMILY LIFE

Families in the region are often large. It is quite common for parents, children, cousins, and grandparents to live close to one another. Grandparents often help by looking after the children when both parents go out to work. However, the situation is changing as young people leave their home areas in search of work in the cities.

In the cities, many people live in modern apartments; some have expensive houses. However, millions of people continue to live in poverty in the shantytowns around large cities such as Lima, La Paz, and Guayaquil. Meanwhile, many indigenous people in the Andes and the Amazon rain forest live in a way that has changed little for centuries.

RELIGION

More than 90 percent of the three countries' combined population are Roman Catholic.

▲ *Every year in Cuzco, the old capital of the Inca empire, a massive festival called Inti Raymi is held, and Andean people celebrate their past.*

MAJOR FESTIVALS AND HOLIDAYS

January 24	ALSITAS (Bolivia; "Puno" in Peru): festival of abundance that dates from Inca times
February/March (week before Lent)	CARNIVAL: lively celebrations in all three countries
May 24	BATTLE OF PINCHIHCHA DAY (Ecuador): celebrating the decisive battle for independence against the Spanish in 1822
June 24	INTI RAYMI: an Inca festival to the Sun God
July 24	Simón Bolívar's birthday (Ecuador): celebrates the birthday of "the Liberator"
July 28 and 29	INDEPENDENCE DAY (Peru)
August 6	INDEPENDENCE DAY (Bolivia)
August 10	INDEPENDENCE DAY (Ecuador)
last week of August	CHU'TILLOS (Bolivia): festival in Potosí celebrating traditional music and dance
October 8	BATTLE OF ANGAMOS (Peru)
November 1 and 2	DIA DE TODOS LOS SANTOS: All Saints' Day
December 24 and 25	CHRISTMAS EVE and CHRISTMAS DAY

◀ *Uros Indians on the floating reed islands on Lake Titicaca combine fishing and other traditional activities with selling items to tourists.*

A small percentage are Protestants. However, many people combine Christianity with ancient beliefs. For example, the Apus, or spirits of the mountains, are still revered by Andean Indians. Amazonian Indians also retain many of their groups' traditional beliefs.

LEISURE

As in most Roman Catholic countries, family occasions such as weddings, birthdays, and christenings are considered very important. Many saints' days are celebrated with processions; some are also marked by national or regional holidays.

In the coastal regions of Peru and Ecuador, people enjoy sunbathing, surfing, and even parasailing on hot summer days. In the Andes, FIESTAS for family occasions or national holidays are often celebrated in a manner that goes back to Inca times. This includes traditional music and dancing, with a meal where meat is cooked in a PACHA MANCA, which is an earth oven made by heating stones.

The most popular sport for men in the region is soccer. The most popular female sport is volleyball. Televisions are not yet common in the countryside, although watching television is an increasingly popular pastime in towns and cities.

◀ *Office workers enjoy a hot cup of coffee during their lunch hour. This is Miraflores, a wealthy suburb of Lima. Miraflores has many recreational facilities, including shopping malls, movie theaters, parks, and a beach.*

► *Many people in La Paz live in slums like this one. Millions of others have moved from the countryside to the cities in the hope of finding work.*

▼ *Bolivian women wait to buy bottled gas for their cooking stoves. Firewood is no longer easy to collect or buy near La Paz.*

SOCIAL PROBLEMS

Peru and Bolivia both have alarming health statistics. In Peru, 47 percent of children of school age suffer from serious malnutrition. Bolivia's infant mortality rate is one of the worst in South America, at 92 deaths per 1,000 live births in 1991, compared with 7 in the U.K. and 9 in the United States. However, Ecuador's health statistics have shown a rapid improvement over the last 30 years. Between 1960 and 1992, the number of patients per doctor in the country fell from 3,000 to 920. This helped raise the life expectancy from 56 to 67 years over the same period.

The region faces many serious social problems. The big gap in wealth between the rich and the poor creates a tension that can often lead to violent crime. In Lima, for example, about half the population lives in shantytowns, in contrast to the very wealthy who have large mansions with swimming pools and servants.

There are also growing numbers of street children. These are mostly children who

The school buildings in rural parts of Ecuador, Peru, and Bolivia are often very basic, such as this one near Iquitos in Peru. Many remote schools in the rain forest areas are run by missionary organizations.

have been abandoned to live on their own in the big cities by parents who do not have enough money to raise them.

One of the most serious problems facing the region is drug trafficking. Peru and Bolivia are the world's largest producers of cocaine. Tons of this illegal drug are transported to the U.S., Canada, and Europe, where addicts are prepared to pay high prices for it.

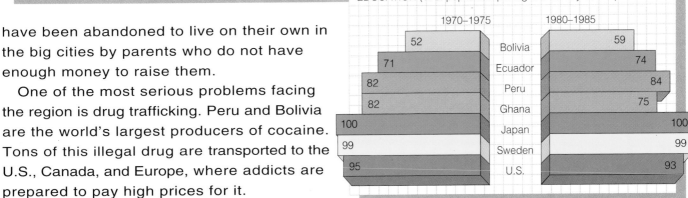

EDUCATION (% of pupils completing elementary school)

	1970–1975	1980–1985
Bolivia	52	59
Ecuador	71	74
Peru	82	84
Ghana	82	75
Japan	100	100
Sweden	99	99
U.S.	95	93

KEY FACTS

● Machu Picchu, the lost city of the Incas, was rediscovered in 1911. It is now the region's top tourist attraction.
● Peru's women's volleyball team is one of the world's best, winning a silver medal in the 1988 Olympics.
● Bolivia's income from the illegal production of cocaine is an estimated 15% of the country's total income.
● Of children who are eligible to enroll for secondary education in Bolivia, only 50% do so.

EDUCATION

Education for children between the ages of 7 and 14 is free and compulsory in all three countries, but many children do not go to school, especially in rural areas. In Bolivia, half of all women living in rural locations cannot read or write, compared with 20% of the population as a whole. The situation is better in Peru and Ecuador, where adult illiteracy stands at about 12%.

The government of Peru has now made education a top priority, spending twice as much money in 1995 than was spent in 1990. Peru has 49 universities, attended by 731,000 students.

All three countries were controlled by Spain until the 19th century, when they gained independence. Today they are all DEMOCRACIES, and since the mid-1980s they have had political stability. However, they have had turbulent histories, with uprisings, military dictators, and land disputes.

Bolivia has fared worst in such disputes. It lost much of its territory, including its coastline, to three of its neighbors in wars between 1879 and 1935.

Peru and Ecuador are still in dispute over land in the Amazon rain forest. They went to war over territories in 1941. In 1942 an "agreement" granted most of the territory to Peru, although Ecuador has never recognized this. The two countries were briefly at war again in 1995.

Under Ecuador's 1978 Constitution, all literate citizens are eligible to vote for a president and vice-president, who serve four years. The government consists of a single chamber of 82 members.

In Peru a new Constitution was approved in 1993. After a five-year term, the

▲ *A statue of Simón Bolívar, "the Liberator" who fought for independence in the region, stands in the center of La Paz, Bolivia.*

KEY FACTS

● President Abdula Bucaram of Ecuador (nicknamed "El Loco") celebrated his election in 1996 by releasing a recording of himself singing "Jailhouse Rock."
● In 1996–1997 the Tupac Amaru terrorist group held 72 people hostage for 4 months in the Japanese Embassy in Lima, Peru.
● In 1994 the government of Bolivia officially recognized the rights of its native people — for the first time since the Spanish conquest in the 16th century.
● Although it is landlocked, Bolivia has a 4,500-strong navy, based on Lake Titicaca.

KEY HISTORICAL EVENTS	The rise of the first major civilization: the Chavin culture in Peru.		Pizarro and the Spanish Conquistadors land on the coast of Ecuador.			War of the Pacific: Peru and Bolivia lose territory to Chile.	
12,000 B.C.	1200 B.C.	200 B.C. – A.D. 1200	1400 – 1532	1530	1821 1825 1830	1879 – 1883	1941
The first people reach South America.		The Tiahuanaco culture flourishes in Bolivia.	The Inca empire is at its peak.		Peru, Bolivia, and Ecuador gain independence.		Peru and Ecuador go to war over a border dispute.

◀ *A tracker dog checks suitcases for drugs. All three countries have problems with drug trafficking.*

president can stand for re-election immediately—which is not the case in Ecuador or Bolivia. There is also a single 120-seat chamber. Voting in elections is compulsory. Any eligible person who does not vote is fined.

Bolivia effectively has two capital cities. Congress is based in La Paz, while the legal capital is Sucre. Under the Constitution of 1967, the president is elected for a four-year term. Congress consists of two chambers: the Senate with 27 seats and the Chamber of Deputies with 130.

▼ *President Fujimori of Peru celebrates his election for a second five-year term in 1995.*

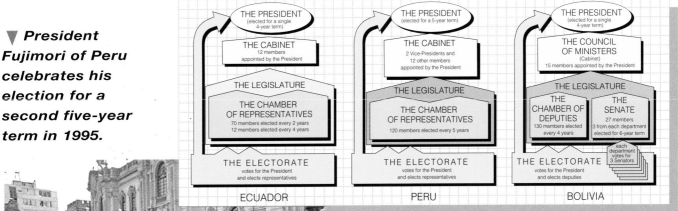

ECUADOR

THE PRESIDENT
(elected for a single 4-year term)

THE CABINET
12 members
appointed by the President

THE LEGISLATURE

THE CHAMBER OF REPRESENTATIVES
70 members elected every 2 years
12 members elected every 4 years

THE ELECTORATE
votes for the President
and elects representatives

PERU

THE PRESIDENT
(elected for a 5-year term)

THE CABINET
2 Vice-Presidents and
12 other members
appointed by the President

THE LEGISLATURE

THE CHAMBER OF REPRESENTATIVES
120 members elected every 5 years

THE ELECTORATE
votes for the President
and elects representatives

BOLIVIA

THE PRESIDENT
(elected for a single 4-year term)

THE COUNCIL OF MINISTERS
(Cabinet)
15 members appointed by the President

THE LEGISLATURE

THE CHAMBER OF DEPUTIES
130 members elected every 4 years

THE SENATE
27 members
3 from each department
elected for 6-year term

each department votes for 3 Senators

THE ELECTORATE
votes for the President
and elects deputies

In all three countries, the electors have to be at least 18 years old. However, in Bolivia people who are not married cannot vote until they are 21.

All three countries have suffered from terrorist activities, such as bombings, killings, and kidnappings. However, Peru's Sendero Luminoso, the most feared terrorist group, has now almost ceased its activities.

FOOD AND FARMING

The agricultural industry employs more than a third of the workers of Peru and Ecuador, and about 60% of Bolivia's workforce. It also makes an important contribution to the countries' economies, earning hundreds of millions of dollars a year. However, many farmers have small plots of land and produce just enough food to feed their families. This is known as SUBSISTENCE FARMING.

Most of the land in the region is not suitable for the cultivation of crops. Only 3% of the total land area of Peru and Bolivia is under cultivation, compared with 9% in Ecuador, but IRRIGATION and the use of the rain forest mean that these figures may rise.

The most intensively farmed areas are the coastal strips of Ecuador and Peru. Large areas of Ecuador's Pacific coastal plains have been drained and grow the bulk of the country's export crops, of which the

► *Thousands of small fish are caught in Lake Titicaca and dried in the sun.*

▲ *Bananas are an important crop in the region. Here they are being loaded for shipment at Riberalta, Bolivia.*

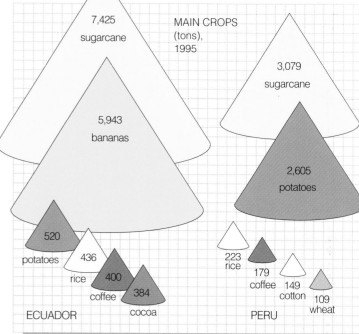

MAIN CROPS (tons), 1995

ECUADOR
- 7,425 sugarcane
- 5,943 bananas
- 520 potatoes
- 436 rice
- 400 coffee
- 384 cocoa

PERU
- 3,079 sugarcane
- 2,605 potatoes
- 223 rice
- 179 coffee
- 149 cotton
- 109 wheat

most important are bananas, coffee, cocoa, rice, and sugar. Ecuador is the world's largest exporter of bananas, which earned them US$ 650 million in export income in 1994. Along Peru's coastal desert, where "high-tech" irrigation techniques are used, the percentage of irrigated land has grown from 3.73% in 1975 to 4.15% in 1993. The principal crops there are cotton, sugar, asparagus, and fruit.

In the Andes most farming consists of tiny farm plots worked by families. Many of the techniques used by subsistence farmers have remained the same for hundreds of years. The main crops are potatoes, corn, beans, and cereals cultivated since Inca times, such as quinoa and kiwicha.

The rain-forested eastern sectors of all three countries have very low population densities and limited agriculture. However, they are the areas that have the greatest agricultural potential. About half of the region's total territory is covered by lowland rain forest, where conditions are excellent

for growing crops such as tea, coffee, and cocoa. The lack of good transport routes has meant that until recently only small quantities of these crops were cultivated. Bolivia has the most developed agriculture in the eastern sector, while cattle ranching has led to a rapid rise in the country's beef exports, especially to Brazil.

The region has enormous potential in terms of timber production, since more than half the total land area is covered by forest. The Amazon Basin is a rich source of

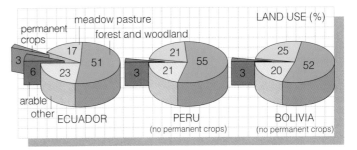

▼ *A field of barley is harvested by hand near Huaraz, Peru. Barley was one of the crops introduced by the Spanish after they conquered the Inca empire.*

BOLIVIA

4,067 sugarcane

1,005 soybean

706 potatoes

143 rice

59 corn

26 coffee

19 cotton

hardwoods such as cedar and mahogany. Other products include rubber and quinine. Bolivia earned US$ 46 million from timber exports in 1992, while Ecuador's exports accounted for US$ 16.5 million in 1993. Most of the 26.4 million cubic feet (7.5 million m^3) of wood harvested in Peru in 1991 were used for firewood or for making charcoal. Only a small proportion was cut into planks.

The fishing industries of Peru and Ecuador are also important. The cold Humboldt Current that sweeps up Peru's coastline creates ideal conditions for fish to breed, although every few years this is replaced by a warm ocean current that causes the fish stocks to fall to almost nothing. However, in good years Peru is second only to China in terms of the size of its fish catch. Anchovies are the main type

◀ *In the Andes, fresh produce is sold in markets such as this one, in the village of Pizac, near Cuzco, in Peru.*

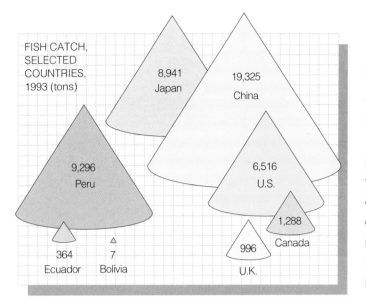

FISH CATCH, SELECTED COUNTRIES, 1993 (tons)

8,941 Japan

19,325 China

9,296 Peru

6,516 U.S.

1,288 Canada

364 Ecuador

7 Bolivia

996 U.K.

▼ *A young man sprays a crop of flowers with a pesticide. Cut flowers from Ecuador and Peru are exported to the U.S. and beyond. This is a thriving industry.*

of fish caught. These and other small fish are chiefly used to produce fish meal. In 1994 the country's fish meal exports were worth US$ 709 million, making them Peru's second most important export, after copper.

Ecuador is South America's largest producer of shrimp and ranks second in the world. The shrimp are cultivated in lagoons cut out of the MANGROVE forests that line the coast. Shrimp are one of Ecuador's three main exports, along with oil and bananas. In 1994 the country's shrimp exports reached a new record of US$ 539 million.

As a landlocked country, Bolivia has a small fishing industry. Lake Titicaca is an important natural fishery that also has commercial trout farms. Most of Bolivia's fish catch is for local consumption.

The staple foods of the local population are potatoes, rice, and corn. Meats such as beef and pork are not part of the general diet, but they are popular on feast days.

KEY FACTS

● 17% of Ecuador's total export income comes from bananas and 16% from shrimp.
● Cut-flower exports earned US$ 54.5 million for Ecuador in 1994.
● Bolivia is the world's second largest exporter of Brazil nuts (after Brazil), producing 6,050 tons (5,500 tonnes) in 1991.
● More than 300 types of potatoes are grown in the Andes.
● About 35% of Peru's total workforce is involved in the farming industry.

TRADE AND INDUSTRY

At the end of World War II in 1945, all three countries had economies based on PRIMARY PRODUCTS (raw materials such as minerals and agricultural produce). These continue to be the mainstay of the three economies, but now there are also industries to process these raw materials. In addition, many other industries have been set up to help reduce the countries' reliance on expensive imports, which include everything from shoes and cars to electronics.

ECUADOR

Ecuador relies on three main exports—oil, bananas, and shrimp. These accounted for 70% of all exports in 1994. This makes the country vulnerable, because the world prices that are paid for these commodities can change at any time.

Since 1965 industrialization has taken off. The first industries to be established in the country included food processing and textiles, taking advantage of Ecuador's excellent agricultural production. In 1993 the food, drink, and tobacco industries still dominated the manufacturing sector of the economy, accounting for 62% of the total value of this sector.

During the 1990s, most industrial growth has been in the manufacture of chemicals, machinery, paper, and the processing of wood products. However, manufacturing exports remain small in comparison with other sectors of Ecuador's economy.

▲ *The Otovalan Indians of Ecuador produce high-quality handicrafts, selling them in stores such as this one, which can be found all over Ecuador. Some items are exported.*

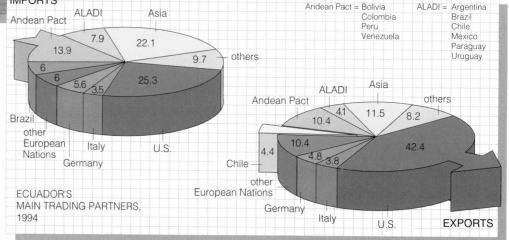

IMPORTS

Andean Pact 13.9
ALADI 7.9
Asia 22.1
others 9.7
Brazil 6
other European Nations 6
Germany 5.6
Italy 3.5
U.S. 25.3

ECUADOR'S MAIN TRADING PARTNERS, 1994

Andean Pact = Bolivia, Colombia, Peru, Venezuela
ALADI = Argentina, Brazil, Chile, Mexico, Paraguay, Uruguay

Andean Pact 10.4
ALADI 4.1
Asia 11.5
others 8.2
Chile 4.4
other European Nations 10.4
Germany 4.8
Italy 3.8
U.S. 42.4

EXPORTS

PERU

Peru has one of the fastest-growing economies in Latin America. There has been steady growth since 1990, and in 1994 the economy grew by 8.6%. This compares with growth of 3.9% in Ecuador.

Today Peru is modernizing its industries. It is also looking more toward the booming Asian countries on the far side of the Pacific as its future trading partners.

As with many other South American countries, Peru depends to a large extent on its natural resources to earn foreign income. For example, mineral exports were worth US$ 1.86 billion in 1994. This was 40.8% of total export income. One of the other major resources is fish. But the fish meal industry is vulnerable to climatic changes, which can cause dramatic declines in the total fish catch.

Peru's main industries are the mining of metals, petroleum, fishing, textiles, clothing, food processing, vehicle assembly, cement, steel, and shipbuilding. Since 1979, the

▲ *High-grade cotton grown on Peru's coastal strip provides one of the main raw materials for the textile industry.*

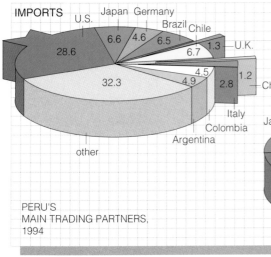

IMPORTS

U.S. 28.6
Japan 6.6
Germany 4.6
Brazil 6.5
Chile 1.3
U.K. 6.7
4.5
4.9 1.2
2.8 China
Italy
Colombia
Argentina
other 32.3

PERU'S MAIN TRADING PARTNERS, 1994

Chile 1.9
China
Italy
Colombia
Argentina
Brazil 4.1
Germany 6.2
Japan 10.3
U.K. 8.9
6.3
4.4
0.5 2.2
16.6
38.6
U.S.
other
EXPORTS

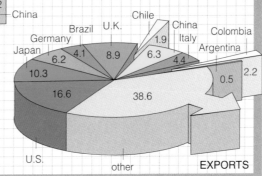

▲ *Thousands of people work at the copper, silver, and lead-smelting plant at La Oroya in the Peruvian Andes.*

fastest-growing industries have been beverages (up by more than 220%), non-metallic minerals (up 158%) and non-industrial chemicals (up 102%).

BOLIVIA

Bolivia is the least industrially developed of all three countries. It relies heavily on mining and minerals such as tin, gold, and antimony, which earned 39% of its export income in 1994. Agricultural exports are also important, with soybeans alone accounting for another 11% of exports.

A new and significant export is natural gas, which is piped to Argentina and Brazil. Argentina is the main customer for the gas, which is fed through a 327-mile (526-km) pipeline. This export was worth about US$ 96 million in 1994. A new 1,387-mile (2,233-km) pipeline is also being built from

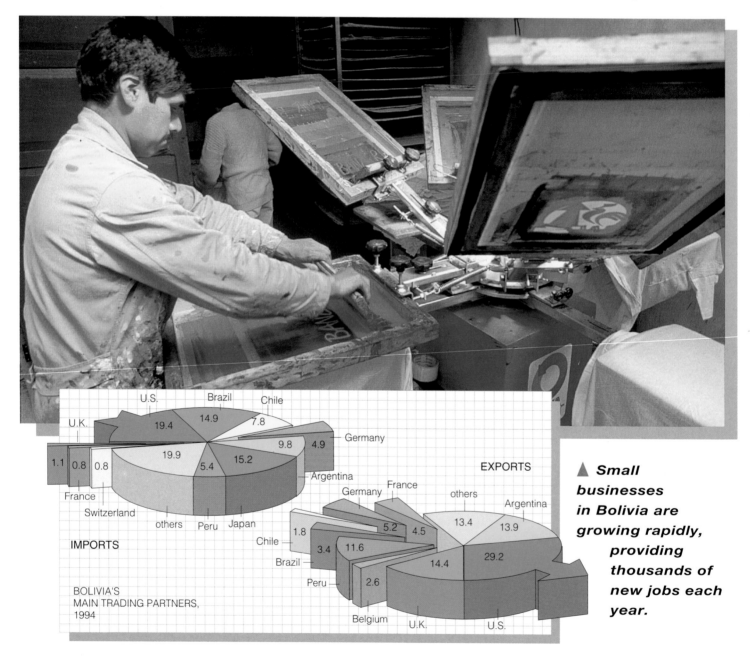

U.S. 19.4   Brazil 14.9   Chile 7.8   Germany 4.9

U.K.   9.8

1.1   0.8   0.8   19.9   5.4   15.2

France   Switzerland   others   Peru   Japan

IMPORTS

BOLIVIA'S MAIN TRADING PARTNERS, 1994

Argentina   Germany   France   others   Argentina

Chile 1.8   Brazil 3.4   11.6   5.2   4.5   13.4   13.9

Peru   2.6   14.4   29.2

Belgium   U.K.   U.S.

EXPORTS

▲ *Small businesses in Bolivia are growing rapidly, providing thousands of new jobs each year.*

KEY FACTS

● Authentic Panama hats are made in Cuenca, Ecuador — not in Panama. They are chiefly exported to the U.S. and Central American countries.

● Ecuador earned US$ 1.185 billion from the export of crude oil in 1995.

● In 1993 Ecuador earned US$ 230 million from tourism, making it the country's fourth largest earner of foreign currency.

● Peru's food industry is dominated by two companies, La Fabril and the Gloria Group.

● Between 1991 and 1995, US$ 400 million was spent on modernizing Peru's fishing fleet.

● Bolivia is the world's fifth-largest producer of tin.

▼ *All three countries have oil industries. This is the base camp for an oil operation in the Amazon Basin.*

Bolivia to the State of São Paulo in Brazil, to start exporting natural gas in 1998.

Manufacturing industries grew slowly in the 40 years after World War II. But since 1984 there has been more rapid growth, especially in the food, drinks, tobacco, and textile industries, which have been responsible for 60% of the new growth. However, in an attempt to cut costs, more than a third of Bolivia's manufacturing workforce lost their jobs between 1984 and 1996.

An important new development is the creation and support of "microindustries." This involves thousands of small businesses producing high-value products. The most successful of these so far has been jewelry. Hundreds of small jewelry businesses had a combined export income of more than US$ 120 million in 1994, 11% of the country's total.

TRANSPORTATION

The varied terrain of Ecuador, Peru, and Bolivia makes communications difficult. The Andes are a formidable barrier between the coastal strips and the eastern lowlands of Peru and Ecuador. This has led to distinct differences in transportation methods between various areas in all three countries.

The best road networks are along the coastal strips of Ecuador and Peru. Excellent paved roads, including the Pan-American highway, run north–south along the coast, linking Guayaquil and places

▼ *Buses in La Paz and other major cities are plentiful and cheap to use. The fares are kept low so that poorer people can afford to travel to work or to a market.*

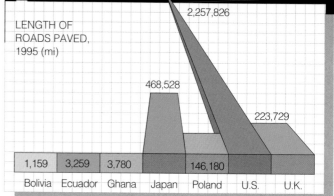

LENGTH OF ROADS PAVED, 1995 (mi)

Bolivia	Ecuador	Ghana	Japan	Poland	U.S.	U.K.
1,159	3,259	3,780	468,528	146,180	2,257,826	223,729

farther north to Lima, and towns as far south as Arequipa. However, only a limited number of roads lead from the coast over mountain passes into the Andes.

The road system in the Andes is poor, since the majority of roads are unpaved. The main forms of transportation for ordinary people are train and bus, which are often overcrowded. The road system in the eastern lowlands is very limited. Only a few roads are usable all year long, because of floods caused by heavy rainfall.

The railroad systems of all three countries are becoming less important for moving raw materials, such as minerals and agricultural produce. In Ecuador only 37,063 tons (33,694 tonnes) of rail freight were carried

◀ *Peru has an impressive network of more than 50 airports. Many are at altitudes of more than 9,842 feet (3,000 m). This is Arequipa Airport, where thousands of tourists arrive every year.*

in 1993. Trains and railroad lines are generally old and in a state of disrepair.

Because of the rough terrain, air travel is extremely important in all three countries. There are more than 50 airports in Peru, while both Quito and La Paz airports handle large amounts of air cargo.

In the eastern sectors of all three countries, the rivers, especially the tributaries of the Amazon, provide the most important transportation system. All the rivers in this area flow away from the capital cities and toward the Atlantic Ocean.

Peru has 21 ports through which the bulk of its produce is exported. Ecuador has four main ports and another two deep-water terminals for oil tankers. However, the port of Guayaquil handles 81% of all non-oil exports. Bolivia has access to seaports only via other countries.

▶ *In the more remote parts of the Andes, people often have to carry goods and basic items themselves or use pack animals. These Canari Indians are taking fodder collected in the mountains back to their animals at home.*

THE ENVIRONMENT

Ecuador, Peru, and Bolivia have a wide range of environments, ranging from deserts to snowcapped mountains, and from lowland rain forests to high altiplano grasslands. Each type of environment faces its own particular problems.

For those close to the big cities and industrial complexes, air pollution has become a serious problem. Vehicles and

▲ *Vicuña are the rarest of the four kinds of camelids that inhabit the Andes (the others are llama, alpaca, and guanaco). These vicuña are protected in a national preserve in southern Peru.*

factories in cities like La Paz, Quito, and Cuzco all produce large quantities of pollutants. These cities are also ringed by mountains, so the pollution does not disperse easily but tends to build up instead. This has caused serious health problems. Coastal cities are also polluted by emissions from vehicles and from industries such as metal-smelting and fish processing. Water contamination is a serious problem, too. The water from Lima's main river, the Rimac, for example, is undrinkable.

Some of the farming methods employed in all three countries are also affecting local environments. Along Peru's coastal strip, industrial farming techniques include irrigation and high chemical usage.

KEY FACTS

● Peru's Manu National Park covers more than 3.7 million acres (1.5 million ha). In one 12-acre (5-ha) plot, scientists have found 10% of all the world's species of birds and 1,000 different types of plants.

● One metal-smelting plant at La Oroya in the Andes has contaminated more than 1.7 million acres (685,000 ha) of farmland with toxic pollutants over the last 30 years.

● About 95% of Ecuador's coastal forests have been destroyed.

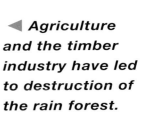

◀ *Agriculture and the timber industry have led to destruction of the rain forest.*

▼ *Tree-planting in some Peruvian reserves helps replace forest and fight soil erosion.*

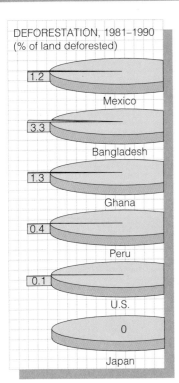

DEFORESTATION, 1981–1990
(% of land deforested)

1.2	Mexico
3.3	Bangladesh
1.3	Ghana
0.4	Peru
0.1	U.S.
0	Japan

Intensive agriculture is rapidly exhausting the soils, while the chemical runoff is polluting rivers and drinking water. Meanwhile, although Peru is the world's second-largest fishing nation, overfishing means that, at current rates, the fish stocks off the coast may be reduced to almost nothing in only a few years' time.

Ecuador's coastal farmlands have also suffered the effects of industrial farming

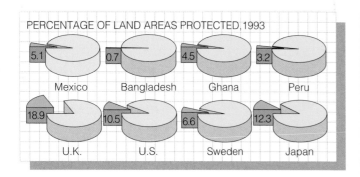

PERCENTAGE OF LAND AREAS PROTECTED, 1993

5.1 Mexico	0.7 Bangladesh	4.5 Ghana	3.2 Peru
18.9 U.K.	10.5 U.S.	6.6 Sweden	12.3 Japan

ECUADOR

Yasuni National Park

Sangay National Park

Pacaya-Samiria National Reserve

PERU

Manu National Park

Tambopata-Candamo Reservation Zone

Noel Kempff Marcado National Park

BOLIVIA

Isiboro-Sécure National Park

Amboró National Park

Galápagos National Park

NATIONAL PARKS

national parks and reserves

0   500 km
     300 mi

N

techniques. Furthermore, intensive shrimp farming has destroyed thousands of acres of mangrove forest since the early 1980s. These were once the breeding grounds of important commercial fish.

The rain-forested lowlands in the east of the region have so far suffered less, although the expansion of farming (such as cattle ranches in Bolivia) is having an impact. Furthermore, the discovery of oil in the Ecuadorean rain forest (in 1972) has led to serious river pollution in an area that supports indigenous people and some of the world's rarest animal and plant species. It is feared that similar problems will occur when new Peruvian and Bolivian oil and natural gas fields are developed.

Many people are aware of the serious environmental problems facing all three countries. They are campaigning to reduce pollution and protect areas of great biological importance. In some cases several local environmental groups have been very successful. For example, in the early 1990s local and international pressure led to the establishment of the Biosphere Reserve of Beni and Yacuma Regional Park, covering a combined area of 1,692,600 acres

◄ *A marine iguana, with a small lizard resting on its head, basks on the rocks of one of the Galápagos Islands.*

▶ *A condor glides over the Colca Canyon in Peru. Condors are the heaviest of all birds of prey and can have a wingspan of more than 10 feet (3 m). These birds are most often seen in the high Andes. They fly along canyons or coastlines in search of food.*

(685,000 ha) in Bolivia.

Governments have a good reason to protect wilderness areas. They attract tourists from all over the world, who contribute millions of dollars to the economy. However, tourism can pose some problems as well. For example, the Galápagos Islands are home to many rare species of plants and animals, and the estimated 60,000 visitors a year are interfering with the islands' fragile environment. There also is a demand to build a new airport there, which would help the economy but destroy part of the environment. The Ecuadorean government has limited development on the islands so far, but some newly arrived islanders want more tourist facilities to be built.

THE FUTURE

Ecuador, Peru, and Bolivia all have great potential for the future. They are rich in natural resources. They also have young populations and are enjoying a period of political stability. At the same time, their economies are growing, and they are ideally placed to develop trade links with the strong economies of Asian countries such as Japan, South Korea, and Malaysia. However, they still face many challenges.

Despite their natural wealth, all three countries have serious social problems. The rural populations of Peru and Bolivia, in particular, experience some of the worst living conditions in South America. However, there have been improvements. For example, life expectancy in Ecuador increased by 11 years between 1960 and 1992.

▲ *President Fujimori of Peru has promised better school facilities, such as computers, to help prepare young people for new types of jobs.*

One major problem facing all three countries is how to provide enough employment for their growing populations. In Peru education has become a top priority, and expenditure on education doubled between 1990 and 1995. With a highly educated workforce, Peru should be able to create large numbers of skilled jobs in manufacturing and processing. Meanwhile, in Bolivia the government is

KEY FACTS

● In 1993 international debts totaled US$ 22.2 billion in Peru, US$ 13.2 billion in Ecuador, and US$ 4.1 billion in Bolivia.
● In 1993–1995 the proportion of people aged under 15 was 35% in Ecuador, 36% in Peru, and 39% in Bolivia.

▶ *Students at La Paz University have decorated the walls of their campus with artwork representing the history and political struggles of Bolivia.*

◀ *In Quito, the capital of Ecuador, the commercial sector of the city has grown in the last few years.*

supporting thousands of small businesses that are creating new jobs and wealth. Ecuador is continuing to develop processing industries to take advantage of its huge natural wealth.

Some of the problems facing the region include drug trafficking, the size of the international debts owed by each country, and the large gap between the rich and the poor. In addition there are environmental problems such as overfishing, air and water pollution, and destruction of rain forests.

However, the future for this interesting region could be very bright. If people's living standards continue to improve, if natural resources are wisely managed, and if problems such as drug trafficking and pollution are confronted, a more secure and productive future should be possible for all.

FURTHER INFORMATION

● Embassy of Bolivia
3014 Massachusetts Avenue, NW
Washington, D.C. 20008

● Embassy of Equador
2535 15th Street, NW
Washington, D.C. 20009

● Embassy of Peru
1700 Massachusetts Avenue, NW
Washington, D.C. 20036

BOOKS ABOUT THE REGION

Lepthien, Emilie U., rev. ed. *Ecuador*. Children's Press, 1993.

McLeish, Ewan. *South America*. Raintree Steck-Vaughn, 1997.

Parker, Edward. *Peru*. Raintree Steck-Vaughn, 1996.

Schimmel, Karen. *Bolivia*. Chelsea House, 1991.

GLOSSARY

ALTIPLANO
A Spanish word for "high plain." It is used to describe the large expanse of level land in the Andes region.

DEFORESTATION
The clearing of trees either so they can be used as fuel, etc., or so that the land can be used for a different purpose, such as farming.

DEMOCRACY
A country that is governed by politicians elected by the people of that country.

EL NIÑO
A warm ocean current that, once every five to ten years, replaces the cold current off the coast of Peru and Ecuador, causing torrential rains to fall over desert lands.

FIESTA
The Spanish word for party or celebration.

FISH MEAL
Dried ground fish that is used for pet food or as a fertilizer.

FOSSIL FUELS
Fuels such as coal, oil, and gas, which are composed of the fossilized remains of plants.

GARÚA
A cool, damp fog that hangs over much of the coast of Peru between April and November.

GEOLOGICAL FAULT
A line of weakness in the Earth's crust, caused by violent movement deep inside the Earth over millions of years. Volcanoes and earthquakes are frequently associated with these areas.

GUANO
An accumulation of bird droppings, rich in nitrates and phosphates, used as a fertilizer.

INDIGENOUS
The original inhabitants of a particular region.

IRRIGATION
An artificial water supply for growing crops.

MANGROVE
Tropical trees that only grow in wet areas. They have distinctive roots that grow out of the water.

MESTIZO
A person of mixed ancestry, who is partly native American and partly European.

OASIS
A fertile spot in a desert where water can be found.

PACHA MANCA
A Quechua (Inca) word meaning an oven in the ground. Typically, rocks are heated over a fire; then food is placed on the rocks, covered with earth, and left to cook for several hours.

PRIMARY PRODUCTS
Things produced that have not yet been processed by industry. They include all types of farm produce, and products of mining and forestry.

SUBSISTENCE FARMING
Producing only enough food for one's family to eat.

TRIBUTARY
A stream or river that flows into a larger river or lake.

INDEX

© Macdonald Young Books
1998